Sir Winston Churchill

Mike Wilson

Published in association with The Basic Skills Agency

Hodder & Stoughton

A MEMBER OF THE HODDER HEADLINE GROUP

Acknowledgements

Photos: pp. iv, 12, 15, 25 © Hulton Deutsch Collection, p. 21 © Alpha/Sport & General, p. 28 © Corbis.

Cover photo: © Popperfoto.

Orders: please contact Bookpoint Ltd, 39 Milton Park, Abingdon, Oxon OX14 4TD. Telephone: (44) 01235 400414, Fax: (44) 01235 400454. Lines are open from 9.00–6.00, Monday to Saturday, with a 24 hour message answering service. Email address: orders@bookpoint.co.uk

British Library Cataloguing in Publication Data
A catalogue record for this title is available from The British Library

ISBN 0 340 72064 6

First published 1994
Impression number 10 9 8 7 6 5 4 3 2 1
Year 2003 2002 2001 2000 1999 1998

Copyright © 1994, 1998 The Basic Skills Agency

Typeset by Fakenham Photosetting Ltd, Fakenham, Norfolk.
Printed in Great Britain for Hodder & Stoughton Educational, a division of Hodder Headline Plc, 338 Euston Road, London NW1 3BH by Page Bros Ltd, Norwich.

Contents

		Page
1	Born to Power	2
2	Young Winston	4
3	Between the Wars	8
4	War	11
5	Churchill's Speeches	13
6	Difficult Decisions	17
7	After the War	21

Late in his life,
Sir Winston Churchill
looked back on his long career.

He said:
'I am not sure
that I have done very well.'

He had not always been popular,
and he had not always been right.

But in 1939, at the age of 65,
he stood up to Adolf Hitler
and Nazi Germany,
and he led Britain to victory
in World War Two.

For this alone he would have
a place in world history.

Many people agree
he is the greatest British statesman
of the twentieth century.

1 Born to Power

Winston Churchill was born
on 30 November 1874.
He was born in Blenheim Palace,
in Oxfordshire.

The Churchills
had been a famous noble family
for hundreds of years.
They had links
with another famous noble family,
the Spencers (Princess Diana's family).
Winston's middle name was Spencer.

Winston's father was
Lord Randolph Churchill,
a top government minister of the day.

His mother, Jennie Jerome,
was a rich American.

Winston was not happy as a boy.
He saw more of his nurse, Mrs Everest,
than he saw of his parents.

He was not very good at school.

In his book, 'My Early Life',
Churchill tells how he passed the exam
to go to public school:

'I wrote my name at the top of the page.
I wrote down the number of the question: 1.
After a while,
I put brackets round it, like that: (1).
But after that,
I couldn't think of anything else to put . . .
My teacher said
I was worthy to pass into Harrow . . .
It was very much to his credit.'

Churchill did not shine at Harrow.
His father decided
he should go into the Army.
But it took young Winston three goes
to pass the entry test.

It was in 1894,
when he was 20,
that Churchill went
to the top Army training college
at Sandhurst.

2 Young Winston

Young Winston spent the next four years
in the Army.
He went to India, then North Africa,
then South Africa.

He spent a lot of time
reading and writing.
He wrote books
and newspaper stories
about the wars he saw.

But he was soon in the news
for his bravery too.
This was in the Boer War,
in South Africa, in 1899.

Churchill was on a train
that was attacked by the Boer soldiers.
He helped save the train,
but was taken prisoner.
But he escaped after a few weeks,
and made his way back to England.

Some years before,
young Winston had sent a letter
to his mother:
'I'd like to come back
and wear my medals
at some big dinner.'

In 1899, he did just that.
When he got back to England,
he got a hero's welcome.

In 1900 Churchill went into politics.
The war hero became a Tory MP.

He was 25,
and he would be in and out of politics
– and in and out of government –
for the next 55 years of his life.

Churchill didn't stay as a Tory MP for long.

In those days,
the other big party
was the Liberals.
In 1904,
Churchill joined the Liberals.

Two years later,
the Liberals won a famous election victory.
Churchill won a place
in the new Liberal government.
He was put in charge of the Board of Trade.

He cut unemployment,
and set up 'Labour Exchanges'
(the first Job Centres)
to help people find work.

He also set a minimum wage.
This was in 1908.

Churchill had vision.
He could see ahead:
what would happen,
or what would be important
in years to come.
Time after time,
he showed this
in his life and work.

He was put in charge
of the British Navy in 1911.

At once, he began building up the Navy.
He feared there would be war
with Germany.
Three years later,
in August 1914,
Britain was at war with Germany.

During the 'Great War',
Churchill left the government
to go and join the Army
fighting in France and Belgium.

Later,
he led a campaign in Turkey.
But the campaign was a flop,
and Churchill was back in government
by 1917.

Back in government,
he helped in making the first tanks,
which broke the German lines
and helped to end the war.

3 Between the Wars

For the next 20 years,
Churchill was in and out of government.
But he was always in the news.

For a time,
he was in charge of the Air Force.

It was Churchill
who put the first British tax on petrol –
four pence a gallon – in 1928.

By this time,
he was back with the Tory Party.

When he joined the Liberals,
he had been called
a traitor to his class.
Now, as the Labour Party grew stronger,
and the Liberals began to fade,
the Tories welcomed him back again.
He was very anti-Labour,
and would be so all of his life.

Churchill was against Communism,
and against the Revolution in Russia.
In the 1920s,
he sent guns and money
to the White Russians,
who were fighting the Red Army.

He was also against Franco,
the Fascist Dictator in Spain
in the 1930s.
But he would not send help
to the anti-Fascist fighters in Spain.

In the early 1930s,
Churchill was one of the only politicians
in Britain who said that
Britain must stand up to Nazi Germany.

All through the 1930s,
Britain and France
let Hitler have his way.
He took over Germany, Austria
and Czechoslovakia.
Britain did nothing.

Churchill did not trust Hitler.
He could see
the Germans would be a danger,
if they got too strong.

Hitler made a peace agreement
with Britain in 1938.
Britain promised to turn a blind eye.
Hitler promised
not to take over any more of Europe.
Churchill called the agreement
'a total defeat,
a defeat without a war.'

He warned:
'Do not suppose that this is the end.
This is only the beginning.'

And he said
Britain should build up the Army,
the Navy and the Air Force
for the war that was bound to come.

Next year,
Britain and Germany were at war.

4 War

On 1 September 1939,
Hitler invaded Poland.
The same day,
Churchill joined the War Cabinet.

The war did not go well
for Britain at first.
Ships were sunk, battles were lost.
Armies were stranded,
and had to be rescued from Dunkirk.

Poland fell to the German armies
in a few hours.
Belgium, Holland
and Norway soon followed.
France fell in a few weeks.
By 1940, Hitler was working on
Operation Sea Lion,
his plan to invade Britain.

The government fell,
and Churchill was asked
to be Prime Minister
for the rest of the war.
He was 65 years old.

5 Churchill's Speeches

From the start,
Churchill gave the British people hope,
even when the future
looked far from hopeful.

This was his very first speech
to Parliament
when he became Prime Minister:

'I have nothing to offer,
but blood, toil, sweat and tears.
You ask: what is our policy?
I will say – it is to wage war,
by sea, by land and air,
with all our might,
and with all the strength
God can give us.
You ask: what is our aim.
I can answer in one word:
Victory!
Victory, in spite of all the terror.
Victory, no matter how long and hard
the road may be.'

Speeches like these gave Britain
the strength to carry on the fight.

As France fell to the Germans,
the French were saying
that Britain would soon follow:

'In three weeks,
England will have her neck wrung
like a chicken.'
Churchill's answer:
'Some chicken. Some neck!'

To the British people he said:
'We shall fight on the beaches,
we shall fight on the landing grounds,
we shall fight in the fields
and in the streets,
we shall fight in the hills;
we shall never surrender.'

To Hitler he said:
'You do your worst,
and we will do our best.'

To America, he said:
'Give us the tools,
and we will finish the job.'

America, the land of Churchill's mother,
had saved Europe in 1917,
when they entered the First World War.
Churchill always knew
that with US money,
Britain could win the Second World War.

So when Japanese planes
bombed US ships
at Pearl Harbor in December 1941,
Churchill knew
America would enter the war.

'So,' he said,
'we have won after all.'

Churchill was right,
but it took another four years.

6 Difficult Decisions

From the beginning of the war,
to the bitter end,
Churchill had to make
some difficult decisions.

At Dunkirk, in 1940,
300,000 soldiers were rescued.
But almost 200,000 had to be left behind.
They were killed,
or became Prisoners of War.

French battleships were bombed
by the British,
so they would not fall into the hands
of the Germans.

In February 1945,
Churchill agreed
to the fire-bombing
of the German town of Dresden.
This was not a military target:
there were no soldiers
or factories there.
The Allies just wanted
to shock the Germans into defeat,
and end the war quicker.

60,000 civilians died in one night.

And then there was Hiroshima.

It was the Americans
who dropped the first atom bomb
on the Japanese city of Hiroshima
on 6 August 1945;
and the second bomb
on Nagasaki three days later.

But Churchill had agreed to it too.

Once again,
the plan was to shock the enemy
into total defeat.

In his 'History of the Second World War',
Churchill wrote:

'There was never a moment's discussion
as to whether the atom bomb
should be used or not.
... to bring the war to an end,
to give peace to the world ...
I did not hear the slightest suggestion
that we should do otherwise.'

130,000 were killed or injured
at Hiroshima
in a matter of minutes.

Within days, Japan surrendered
and the war was over.

Crowds celebrate the end of World War II.

7 After the War

The Allies had won the war,
but what would peace be like?

A new world
was rising from the ashes
of the old world.

Churchill wrote:
'When the war of the giants is over,
the wars of the pygmies begin.'

He used the words 'Cold War'
and 'Iron Curtain'
to explain the new Europe
that he saw being born.

He had saved the world from Hitler
and the Nazis.
But now Europe was at the mercy
of America and Russia.

In 1946, he made a speech:
'We must build
a United States of Europe.'

This idea was years ahead of its time.
But he knew it wouldn't work.
He knew Russia and America
would never give up
the power they had won in 1945.

The Cold War lasted 40 years.
The Russians and Americans
spent billions on the Arms Race.
Europe lay in the shadows,
split in two by the 'Iron Curtain'.

This was what Churchill was thinking,
way back in the dark hours of 1940,
when he made speeches
about victory over the Nazis:
Victory at all costs!

After the war, in 1945,
there was a general election
in Britain, and Labour won.

Churchill had to quit as Prime Minister.

It was a bitter disappointment –
he won the war,
but lost the election.

But he was back in power
from 1951 to 1955.
In that time
he at last got rid of rationing
for the first time since the war.

By 1955, Churchill was 80.

He had become
Sir Winston Churchill in 1953.
That same year,
he had his first major stroke.
Yet the old man still hung on to power.

He told Parliament:

'It's not for the love of power or office.
I've had my share of both.
It's because
I feel I still have something to offer
in the building
of a sure and lasting peace.'

But the truth was
the old man did not think much
of the man who was to take his place.

Sir Anthony Eden
took over as Prime Minister
in April 1955.

And within two years,
following the Suez Crisis,
Eden resigned,
a sick and a failed man.

After Churchill retired, aged 80,
he lived quietly.
He spent his time writing.

He wrote a history
of the Second World War.
And he won the Nobel Prize
for his book:
'The History of the English Speaking Peoples'
(1956–58).

And the man who
had been such a friend of America;
who had called for America
to join in two World Wars
was made an honorary US citizen
in 1963.

Churchill died, aged 90,
in January 1965.
He had another stroke,
and died quietly in his bed.

He was given a state funeral
in St Paul's Cathedral,
and was buried with his family
near Blenheim Palace,
where he had been born.

When Churchill was born,
men still fought on horses,
using swords and pistols.

When he died,
they used rockets and atom bombs.

Most people agree
that Sir Winston Churchill
saved his country in time of need.

We remember how brave he was,
how brave he made us feel,
in the dark days of war.
We remember his words:
'This was their finest hour.'